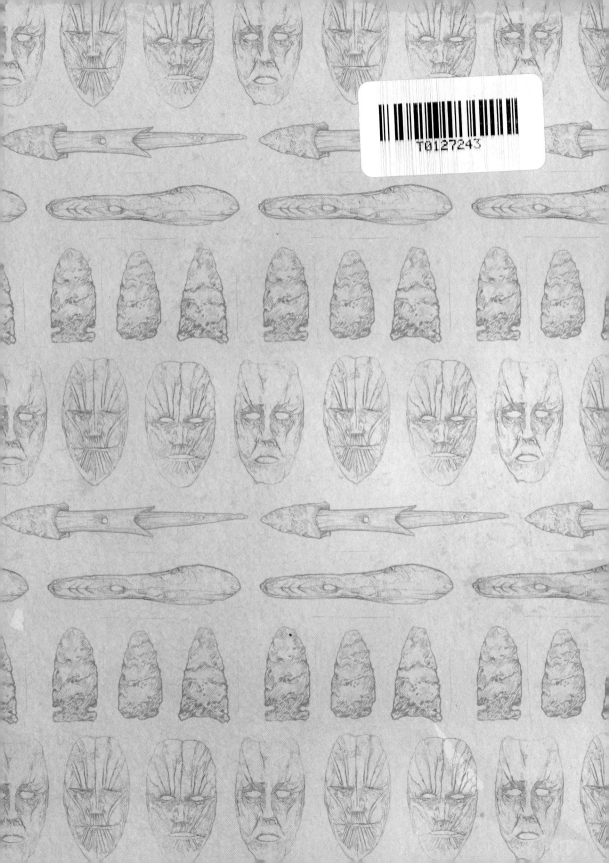

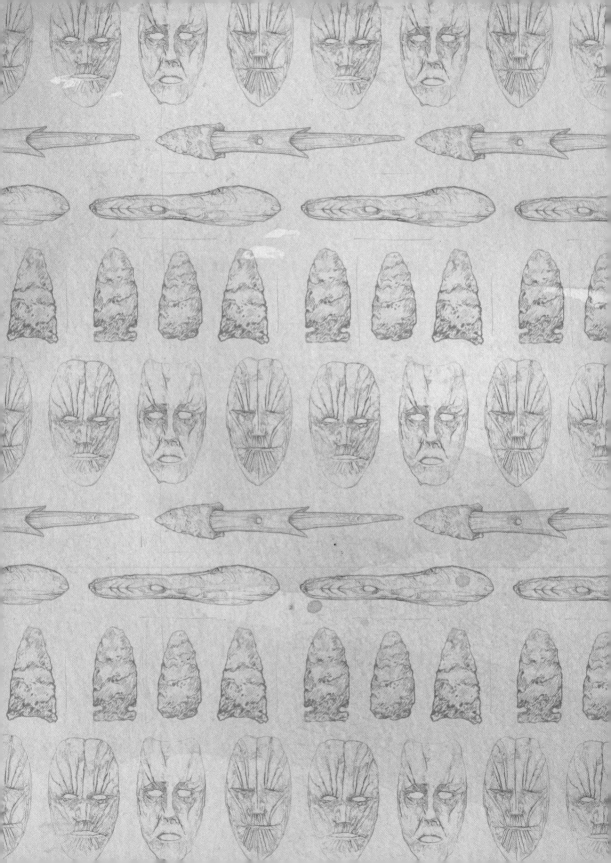

TUNIIT

Mysterious Folk of the Arctic

by Rachel and Sean
Qitsualik-Tinsley

Illustrated by
Sean Bigham

INHABIT
MEDIA

Published by Inhabit Media Inc.
www.inhabitmedia.com

Inhabit Media Inc. (Iqaluit), P.O. Box 11125, Iqaluit, Nunavut, X0A 1H0
(Toronto), 146A Orchard View Blvd., Toronto, Ontario, M4R 1C3

Design and layout copyright © 2014 Inhabit Media Inc.
Text copyright © 2014 Rachel and Sean Qitsualik-Tinsley
Illustrations by Sean Bigham copyright © 2014 Inhabit Media Inc.

Editors: Neil Christopher and Louise Flaherty
Art director: Danny Christopher

We acknowledge the financial support of the Government of Canada through the Department of Canadian Heritage Canada
Book Fund.

We acknowledge the support of the Canada Council for the Arts for our publishing program.

Printed in the United States of America

Canadian Patrimoine
Heritage canadien   Canada   Canada Council   Conseil des Arts
for the Arts   du Canada

Library and Archives Canada Cataloguing in Publication

Qitsualik-Tinsley, Rachel, 1953-, author
        Tuniit : mysterious folk of the Arctic / by Rachel and
Sean Qitsualik-Tinsley ; illlustrated by Sean Bigham.

ISBN 978-1-927095-76-8 (bound)

        1. Inuit-Canada-Juvenile literature. 2. Canada, Northern-
Antiquities-Juvenile literature. I. Qitsualik-Tinsley, Sean, 1969-,
author II. Bigham, Sean, illustrator III. Title.

E99.E7Q286 2014   j971.9004'9712   C2014-905068-2

TUNIIT

Mysterious Folk of the Arctic

Table of Contents

1

Inuit and Tuniit: Two Arctic Peoples

Inuit use a word to describe what is now Canada's Arctic: *nalunaqtuq*. The word means "uncanny" or "unpredictable." Basically, it means that the Arctic is always shifting. Always changing. You never know when a snowstorm is going to hit. You never know when the ice is going to give way under your feet. Because the sea freezes solid in the long, dark winters, hunters feed their families by going out to hunt on the ice. But even the most experienced hunters have encountered the threat of ice pans breaking off—without the hunter even knowing it—and floating away, hunter and all. Hunters have even tried to find their way home through blinding snowstorms, only to have the weather suddenly clear, and find that they were standing a stone's throw away from their own homes!

Inuit love the Arctic, but they know not to trust it. And they're not just nervous about the weather. Many still believe in magical creatures that might hide behind every stone, in every ice crack, or far out beyond the sound of engines.

The past—especially the ancient past—was just as nalunaqtuq as the present. We even have scientific proof that the Arctic used to be full of unlikely animals. Giant camels, for instance. Mammals similar to rhinos and hippos. Dinosaurs with giant eyes and night vision for hunting in the winter darkness. The Inuit language, Inuktitut, still has words for the huge beavers that used to live here. It has words to describe a woolly mammoth!

And it has a word to describe the people who came before Inuit.

These people were the *Tuniit*: the folk that Inuit encountered when they first moved into what is now Arctic Canada and Greenland. Maybe you're wondering whether these Tuniit folk are some of the magical beings that Inuit feared. Or whether they were real, like the camels.

The answer is yes, and yes. Tuniit are very special beings, because they blend the realms of Inuit myth and fact. Scientists say that they existed. But if we go by what Inuit stories have to say about them, the Tuniit were anything but normal people.

Understanding Tuniit and Tuniq

Keep reading and you'll come across two words to describe these mysterious Arctic beings. You've already read one such word: Tuniit. The other is *Tuniq.* Tuniq is simply the singular form of Tuniit, since Tuniit describes a bunch of these odd beings.

We take note of how to properly say things, since choice of language is all about respect. For example, we all know who the Inuit are (the people who used to be called Eskimos), but we shouldn't go around saying, "Inuits." One of the Inuit is simply an Inuk.

But what do Tuniit and Tuniq mean? No one is quite sure, since Inuit started using these words a long time ago. Words are just spoken ideas. And ideas can be like keepsakes that you've put away in storage for too long: you can easily forget where you placed them.

Maybe "Tuniit" is a unique word. Maybe it's a word from the Tuniit themselves. And since we can't ask the Tuniit about their language, we'll never know for sure.

It's possible, though not proven, that "Tuniq" is related to words like "*tuniqruti.*" The root means "something given." If that's true, then "Tuniit" might mean something like "Givers." This might make sense, since the Tuniit were said to have taught the first Inuit about the new lands they were moving into. But maybe the word is related to "*tunirijaq,*" which means "flint." This could also make sense, since the Tuniit were said to have made a lot of spearheads and arrowheads from flint.

Were Tuniit Human or Not?

There are plenty of Inuit stories about the Tuniit. Most describe them as possessing strange powers, some of which make us question whether or not they were actually human beings.

Tuniit (the men, at least) are often described as beastlike, and there are some rare tales that describe them as covered in hair. Other tales, ones recorded from Inuit elders speaking as far back as the 1920s, depict Tuniit speaking with a strange "hom, hom" sort of noise, in a jerky way, as though there was something alien about their voices.

Elders and scientists alike seem to agree, though, that Inuit were able to communicate with Tuniit. Maybe the "hom" sound that has been recorded in Inuit tradition was supposed to imply that the Inuit and Tuniit languages were alike, but not quite the same.

One of the oddest details about the Tuniit is the difference between men and women. Inuit legends all agree that the Tuniit men were very short. One story even goes so far as to claim that their hunting tools were too big for them, dragging on the ground as they walked!

Tuniit women, however, looked like normal Inuit women, and were supposedly very lovely. This caused trouble from time to time, since Inuit men sometimes became obsessed with Tuniit women. A few Inuit men even tried to kidnap such women. Whenever this happened, there was trouble. The Tuniit men may have been short, but they were far from helpless.

Tradition tells us that only one Tuniq, a man named Tillussuaq, once turned the tables on Inuit by kidnapping an Inuk woman. But the poor Tuniq fell in love with her. When she was accidentally killed in a raid by vengeful Inuit, he howled out a song in his grief. His death-song broke the hearts of those Inuit hearing it, so that they remembered the words forever after in their own stories.

Tuniq man   Tuniq woman

Sometimes it seems as though there are too many stories about
Tuniit! Some tales seem to contradict each other. Were the Tuniit
skilled craftsmen or very sloppy? Were they good-looking or
frightening to behold? When talking about the Tuniit, we have to
focus on the details that stories agree upon.

Inuit and Tuniit: Differences and Similarities

Tuniit flint blade

Science and Inuit tradition seem to agree on one thing: the big difference between Inuit and Tuniit was technology. The Tuniit made most of their tools out of flint. Their carving was basic, just enough to make useable tools for hunting large animals.

Inuit, however, carried a very fine toolkit: slender little probes and picks, and well-carved toggles and barbs. They did not always feel it necessary to use flint. Since Inuit hunted a greater variety of animals than the Tuniit did, Inuit tools were made from antler, whalebone, baleen, and ivory from narwhals and walruses. It seems that the Tuniit rarely used bows and arrows, while Inuit depended on strong, sinew-backed bows, often made from whalebone.

Inuit legends insist that the Tuniit had a great love of their homes. There came a time when the Tuniit were pushed out of their lands by Inuit. One of the Tuniit was so upset at having to leave his home that he plunged his spear into a stone. The blow was so powerful that the rock itself shattered, sending out a spray of stone chips in every direction!

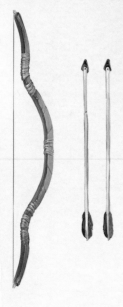

Inuit bow and arrow

Everything about the Inuit lifestyle said "keep moving." Inuit were nomads, strangers, when they first explored North America's Arctic.

Yet everything about the Tuniit lifestyle said "stay in place."

For example, Tuniit tended to build stone shelters, some of them quite large. They had small sleds, but there is no evidence that they owned any dogs. It seems that the Tuniit pulled their sleds themselves. If you have ever pulled a sled, you know that it can get a bit tiring. Now imagine pulling a sled loaded down with a big bull caribou!

Even though both scientists and Inuit legends agree that Inuit had better technology than the Tuniit did, Inuit stories insist that the Tuniit taught early Inuit a lot about hunting techniques. In fact, the Tuniit had one unique item of hunting technology that they depended on, and Inuit still use it to this day: the *inuksuk*.

Tuniq man pulling caribou on a sled.

Inuit used dogsleds for travel in all but the warmest summer months. Dogs were—and still are—so important to Inuit life that a good hunter always knew the finer points of dog breeding. Inuit families tended to shelter in a small, temporary snow house, called an *iglu*, or a tent called a *tupiq*. Even when early Inuit created art, they tended to combine it with some sort of tool (like a bear's head carved into a spoon, for example), so that it would serve a useful purpose in addition to being beautiful. That way, they could pack everything onto a dogsled without being weighed down by unnecessary belongings.

Inuksuk

Most Inuit stories seem to be careful not to make the Tuniit look unintelligent. Instead, they simply emphasize how odd the Tuniit way of life seemed to Inuit. That's a danger any of us can run into, when we're too used to our own culture. Another way of life may look a bit foolish, when it is really just adapted to a different lifestyle. The Tuniit simply had their own ways of hunting, surviving, and understanding the world. And these would have seemed pretty odd to Inuit.

Do you know what an inuksuk is? You've probably seen one. Maybe you've noticed a tiny one in a gift shop. Or seen a full-sized one in somebody's garden. If you're very lucky, you've seen a real inuksuk.

An inuksuk is a standing pile of rocks, usually about waist high. It's built so that arms seem to stick out at the sides. A round stone at the top looks a bit like a head. Think of it as a snowman made of stones.

The Tuniit used to build *inuksuit* (the plural of inuksuk) on the tops of hills, so that their outlines could be seen against the sky. The idea was to make it look like people stood on the hilltops. If a herd of caribou saw such shapes, they would avoid them. With enough inuksuit in place, the Tuniit could make caribou run in whichever direction they wanted them to go. Then the Tuniit hunters could plan an ambush.

Legend tells us that the Tuniit taught this hunting technique to the first Inuit who came into the eastern Arctic.

Tradition tells us that Tillussuaq, the last Tuniq of Iqaluit, used to scare Inuit half to death by hunting with stones. Tillussuaq was small compared to other Tuniit. But using simple stones, he could crush the skulls of polar bears and walruses.

2

What Makes Tuniit Special?

—⁘—

Strength

Of all the things that Tuniit were known for, their strength was the most amazing. It was said that Tuniit could lift boulders many times their own size. And to this day, at various sites around the Arctic, there are great rocks that Inuit claim were placed there by Tuniit.

When a male Inuk would kidnap a female Tuniq, as they are often said to have done, it always went badly for the kidnapper. Such Inuit men usually ended up crushed to death. In one traditional tale, an Inuk hunter is caught by his wrists, and the Tuniq holding him is so strong that he accidentally breaks the hunter's arms!

The strength of the Tuniit was said to be so great, in fact, that they did not always need spears to kill their prey. It is said that if they caught their prey by running it down, which stories tell us they *could* do, they could snap the neck of even a bull caribou by simply wrestling with it.

Speed

Not only were the Tuniit strong—they were fast, for that was how they hunted. If they wanted an animal, they would simply go get it. Coupled with their strength, the Tuniit's speed made them potentially deadly to just about anything they laid eyes on. And their speed was not simply like that of a cheetah, which tires after its initial quick sprint. Traditional stories tell us that the Tuniit could run for days without tiring. Running was so important to them that they even slept with their legs sticking up in the air, supposedly to keep their feet light.

Shifting Size and Weight

Many stories mention another bizarre power that the Tuniit are said to have possessed. According to legend, they could make themselves heavy or light at will. Some could even change their size, becoming as small or huge as they needed to be in order to accomplish a given task.

In one story, an Inuit hunter is paddling in his *qajaq* (a one-man boat) when he comes across a Tuniq trapped on an ice pan. The Tuniq explains that he is adrift, helpless, as he has managed to lose his own boat (the Tuniit are sometimes depicted as being a bit absent-minded). The Tuniq asks the hunter for a lift back home. When the hunter asks how they'll both fit into his little qajaq, the Tuniq just laughs.

"Ha!" he chuckles. "I forgot that humans can't change their weight!"

Becoming light as feather, the Tuniq hops onto the qajaq and holds on while the hunter paddles him home.

Shyness

There are only three things that all tales about Tuniit agree upon. The first is that Tuniit were short. The second is that they were strong.

The third is that they were shy.

Not only were the Tuniit shy, they were *painfully* shy. When Inuit first came into the eastern Arctic in their skin boats and on their dog-sleds, Tuniit were supposedly a common sight. But contact with the Tuniit remained rare. This was because Tuniit tended to run for the hills at the very sight of Inuit.

In their traditional tales, Inuit usually paint themselves as the aggressors against Tuniit. It is Inuit who try to confront Tuniit. It is Inuit who attack or scare off Tuniit if their presence becomes inconvenient. And it is Inuit who steal from Tuniit. Usually, if an Inuk is hurt or killed by a Tuniq in a traditional story, it is by accident or in self-defense.

This depiction is strange, if you stop to consider it. You would think, with all the marvellous abilities the Tuniit were said to possess, that it would be Tuniit who would pose a threat to Inuit. It would make sense that Inuit, as strangers in a strange land, would be vulnerable. They would be meeting a people whom their own tales insist are faster, stronger, and far more powerful than they.

Yet the Tuniit, it seems, had no interest in fighting.

Overall Strangeness

To this day, many Inuit believe that a kind of magic runs through Land, Sea, and Sky. As recently as decades ago, it was believed that special people called shamans (*angakkuit* in Inuktitut) could access the secret powers running through the world, using them to harm or heal.

It was believed that the Tuniit, in particular, were powerful shamans. How common were shamans in their society? Apparently common enough that Tuniit tales are filled with incredible magic. One tale tells of how a feeble old Tuniq man grows cranky with the cold storm winds blowing down on him. He stands up just long enough to sing a little song to the storm. As a result, the Sea and Sky grow calm for as far as the eye can see.

Besides their amazing strength and speed, and their legendary ability to change size and weight, the Tuniit were known for being generally odd. At least by Inuit standards. Despite the fact that their tools were poor, stories tell that their clothing was of exceptional quality. Their coats were said to be very odd, though. They were overly long and often covered in duck feathers!

Like Inuit, the Tuniit sometimes stayed warm by burning seal oil in a tiny stone lamp. But while Inuit kept large soapstone lamps at the centre of their homes, Tuniit hunters were said to carry tiny stone lamps inside their own coats. Most of the time, however, the Tuniit stayed warm by burning lots of Arctic heather. If you've ever burned Arctic heather, you'll already know that it produces an incredible amount of smoke. For that reason, Inuit sometimes called the Tuniit the "Sooty Ones."

The list of Tuniit eccentricities goes on and on: sleeping with their feet pointing up in the air, speaking with an unusual rhythm, wearing their hair in strange topknots, sewing murre-skin mitts and polar bear-skin pants, exhibiting confusing behaviour, and having many tattoos . . . .

Tradition tells us that Tuniit around the area of Iqaluit were not as shy as the Tuniit Inuit typically encountered. After a while, a couple of Tuniit even realized that they could have some fun by deliberately scaring the Inuit!

Tuniit are not the only beings that Inuit described as wearing clothes covered in duck feathers. Inuit seem to have used the idea of wearing eider duck coats to indicate anyone or anything that was odd. In some stories, the *qallupiluq*, a kidnapping monster that lives in watery ice cracks, is also said to wear such clothing. This idea might have come from the fact that small, isolated groups of people related to Inuit really did have eider duck coats

Qallupiluq

Some elders have used the expression "*Nunaup Sanngininga*" to describe the power running through the Land. It means the "Strength of the Land." In this case, Land means the entire world, including its unseen corners. This power was tapped into by shamans and sometimes by ordinary people. But it was not spiritual, nor was it worshipped. Instead, it was like an alternative science, activated by willpower and words—including songs that were passed down through generations. So, shamans were not really priests or wizards. They were important to ancient Inuit—and especially to Tuniit, it seems—in the same way that scientists, technicians, and doctors are important to modern cultures.

In comparison with First Nations peoples (who used to be incorrectly called "Indians"), colonial visitors made contact with Inuit very late: about 400 years later, to be exact. For this reason, Inuit got to enjoy their traditional way of life up until very recently. As late as the 1950s, there were still many families who lived a nomadic way of life, hunting entirely by dogsled and without rifles. Consequently, the old way of life is well remembered, and is currently being catalogued before important elders can pass away. Living Inuit still have their language, Inuktitut, and still remember their ancient beliefs—including those about Tuniit.

3

What the Sciences Have to Say

We know that there were definitely cultures in the North American Arctic before Inuit arrived. From the far west (what is now Alaska) to the far east (what is now Labrador and Greenland), the Arctic is littered with artifacts. There are old stone rings where tents once stood. There are ancient fire pits and garbage heaps. There are a few gravesites, and even a few skeletons.

Mostly, there are items from everyday life: arrowheads, spearheads, barbs, carvings, combs, toggles, needles, goggles, toys, and every kind of tool for cutting, gouging, drilling, scooping, and scraping.

We know that Inuit used most of these things. From the time that European visitors, or "colonials," first began to arrive in the Arctic, they began to record what they saw of Inuit life. They passionately collected the artifacts they found—perhaps a bit too passionately, going so far as to remove objects from graves.

In their obsession with collecting and cataloguing everything they found, however, the colonial visitors began to realize a startling fact—not all of the artifacts were left by Inuit!

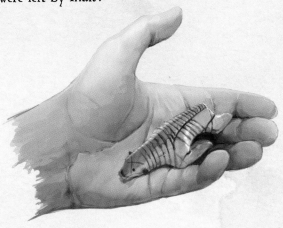

Two Strange but Important Words: Dorset and Thule

Most of the people who collected Arctic artifacts simply hoarded them. Many artifacts sit forgotten in boxes or as private exhibits to this day.

But in 1925, a few artifacts from the pre-colonial Arctic found their way to a very famous anthropologist named Diamond Jenness. Jenness soon realized that he was not looking at Inuit artifacts, but at the leavings of a folk who were quite different from Inuit, and who had lived in the region long before Inuit arrived. Perhaps not knowing that Inuit already knew about this folk—and that they called them Tuniit—Jenness labelled his mystery culture "Dorset."

So, under Jenness and other scientists, a hunt began to study and understand this Dorset culture. Along the way, Jenness distinguished the Tuniit/Dorset from Inuit by labelling the ancestors of Inuit the "Thule" culture.

Jenness and other scientists never painted the Inuit as much different from their Thule ancestors. They always admitted that Inuit have changed very little since the time their ancestors first moved into North America's eastern Arctic—this may be why Inuit still remember so much history through their stories! Basically, we might say that "Dorset" is just a way of saying "historical, rather than mythological, Tuniit." "Thule" is a way of saying "Inuit before they finished settling across the Arctic."

Discovering Distant Cousins

As Arctic anthropology unfolded, it was discovered that an entire cross-cultural drama had unfolded over nineteen centuries or more. Stone and rare scraps of metal are hard to date. But the Arctic cold preserves organic material—that is, anything that comes from a once-living creature—very well. Luckily, both the Tuniit/Dorset and Inuit/Thule cultures used a lot of organic material, especially in the form of antler, bone, and ivory tools. These organic artifacts are easy to date.

Earth has never been a stable home. The planet's temperatures often shift and wobble like a top spinning off its axis. Scientists have discovered that it turned very cold about 2,800 years ago. Humans were already in the Arctic then, and they had to adjust to the new temperatures by developing a very

specific lifestyle. Thus began the Tuniit/Dorset culture.

The planet didn't stay that cold, though. It took a while to warm, but when it did, about sixteen centuries later, some Alaskan peoples got the urge to travel. They, too, had developed their own specific culture. These were the Inuit/Thule people, and they spread eastward—all the way to Greenland—as the planet warmed between 1,200 and 800 years ago. Evidence tells us that before the planet grew cold again, they encountered and eventually replaced the Tuniit/Dorset people who had become so well settled in the eastern Arctic. During these few centuries, Inuit could not have realized a fact that science uncovered: the Tuniit shared ancestry with the Inuit. That is, the Tuniit, too, had once been part of a migration coming out of Alaska (although a migration much more ancient than that of Inuit).

In other words, Inuit and Tuniit were distant cousins.

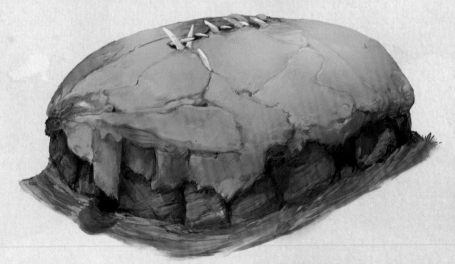

As it turned out, scientists discovered that there was a basis for many of the Inuit beliefs about Tuniit. The Tuniit, for example, did show some evidence of settled life. Scientists discovered their stone "longhouses," just as they were described in Inuit stories. It was initially suggested that such longhouses were evidence of Viking settlements, but that theory was disproven. Also, Tuniit artifacts are very much geared toward the use of shamanism, lending strength to Inuit claims that the Tuniit were powerful shamans. Most mysterious of all: the Tuniit loved faces. They left behind many images of faces, carved or painted onto boulders across the Arctic. As to what these faces meant, we may never know—because we have no Tuniit to interview.

What Happened to the Tuniit?

From the time that Inuit moved into traditional Tuniit lands, it seems that the Tuniit began disappearing. Both science and Inuit tradition agree on this. No one, however, knows exactly why the Tuniit disappeared.

Some opinions point to stories of conflict between Tuniit and Inuit, suggesting that maybe Inuit exterminated all of the Tuniit. Other sources, including stories of Tuniit and Inuit intermarrying, suggest that the two peoples simply blended together. If this is true, then it is the culture of the Tuniit that has gone extinct, while the Tuniit genes now reside within those who call themselves Inuit.

Some have suggested that the last true population of Tuniit might have included the unique and shy folk who once populated what are now Southampton Island and Coats Island. In the late 1800s, however,

both populations were contacted by sailors who brought plague to their community. By the time another ship visited in 1902, the islands were barren. Decades later, in 1954, anthropologist Henry B. Collins studied the stone house ruins of the islands. He declared them to represent the last of the Dorset culture.

Inuit have a particularly creepy legend about the end of the Tuniit. A story claims that there rose from the waters a race of creatures called the *Ikuutarjuit*. These creatures were known as "the drillers." Their delight was in ambushing Tuniit hunters while they paddled on the sea. Inuit depicted them as black and oily, like something between a cod and an eel. These demons killed the Tuniit by drilling holes in their skulls. While the Tuniit were exterminated by the drillers, a lone Inuk eventually drove the creatures back into the sea.

All That Remains

Myth and legend can seem hazy. Like dreams. But, also like dreams, they can inspire.

So, remembering Inuit legends, Brian Pearson of Iqaluit established a spring festival that honours that fierce and tragic figure: Tillussuaq, the last Tuniq of Iqaluit.

The yearly festival was established in 1965. Since that time, it has blossomed into an important time during which Inuit welcome the return of light and warmth after winter's long darkness. The festival is called Toonik Tyme. At its symbolic height, the title of "Honorary Toonik" (an old-fashioned way of spelling Tuniq) is awarded to one person whom the community wishes to recognize. In the past, this honour has been bestowed upon leaders of countries. Even visiting princes!

It is important to remember, though, that under Toonik Tyme's culture of joy, there runs a dark nod to the extinct Tuniit. This festival is like a long moment of silence, as are ancient stories about Tuniit. Remembrance through lore is one of the few ways in which we can respect the Tuniit. We remember a fate that no culture should have to endure.

We must not remember simple myths, however. We must remember the Tuniit as those who inspired myths, but who were real humans. All of our evidence, whether science or story, tells us that these strange Arctic people loved their families. Their ways of life. Their homes.

Mysterious or not, if any of us want to be remembered, it is through what we love.

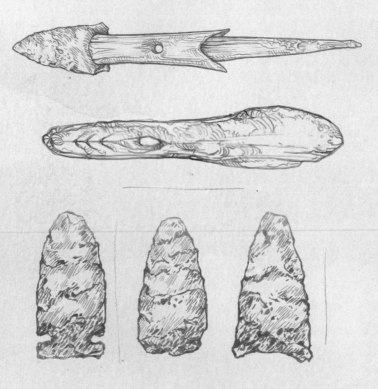

Dorset artifacts

Further Reading

Canadian Arctic Prehistory by Robert McGhee

Eskimo Folk-Lore by Diamond Jenness

Eskimo Folk-Tales by Knud Rasmussen (archived at Sacred Texts Archive; www.sacred-texts.com/nam/inu/eft/)

"In the Bones of the World" (articles I-IX, by Rachel A. Qitsualik; archived by *Nunatsiaq News* www.nunatsiaqonline.ca)

Inuktitut: A Multi-Dialectal Outline Dictionary by Alex Spalding

Shamanism: Archaic Techniques of Ecstasy by Mircea Eliade

The Netsilik Eskimo by Asen Balikci

Toonik Tyme Iqaluit (website: www.tooniktyme.com)

Ulirnaisigutiit by Lucien Schneider

Contributors

Born in an Arctic wilderness camp and of Inuit ancestry, Rachel Qitsualik-Tinsley is a scholar specializing in world religions and cultures. Her numerous articles and books concerning Inuit magic and lore have earned her a Queen Elizabeth II Diamond Jubilee Medal.

Of Scottish-Mohawk ancestry, Sean Qitsualik-Tinsley is a folklorist and fantasist, specializing in mythology, magic, and Inuit lore. He has won an award for writing short science fiction ("Green Angel"), but his focus is on fiction and non-fiction for a young audience.

Sean Bigham is an artist based out of London, Ontario. He works in the video games industry as a concept artist. Sean attended the Alberta College of Art and Design. *Tuniit: Mysterious Folk of the Arctic* is his first book.

INHABIT
MEDIA